Alan Titchmarsh's  Gardening Guides

HEALTHY HOUSE PLANTS

HAMLYN

London · New York · Sydney · Toronto

Finding a healthy plant

A house plant that's bristling with health and full of energy when you buy it will give you a head start when it comes to keeping it happy at home, so it makes sense to shop around for the best.

You'll find house plants on sale in all sorts of places, but here's a list of where to buy them, given in order of preference:

- The nursery where the plant was grown
- A garden centre
- A chain store or supermarket
- A greengrocer's shop

The idea is to get the plant home with as little shock to its system as possible. Buy from a nursery or garden centre and the plant will have been well cared for and is unlikely to have caught a chill.

Buy from a supermarket or chain store only if the plants are fresh (look for the week number on the wrapper). Buy from a greengrocer's only as a last resort, especially in winter. House plants come from warm countries and don't enjoy draughty December days on British pavements.

With Christmas pot plants you've no option but to buy in winter; other pot plants can be more safely transported home in spring and summer when temperatures are higher and they are growing more rapidly.

Whatever the time of year, insist that the plant is well wrapped up. Get it home as quickly as possible, and don't leave it to freeze or fry in the car.

What makes a good plant?

Biggest doesn't always mean best in the house plant world.

Look for a plant that has:

- A good shape
- No browning at the leaf tips
- No pests
- Moist compost around the roots
- A perky appearance

Avoid plants that have:

- Wilting leaves
- Greenfly or other pests
- Disease-spotted leaves
- Dry and shrunken compost
- Bare stems
- Any kind of damage

If you're buying a flowering plant, choose one that has some blooms fully open and some in bud. Plants in full flower may fade quickly; those in tight bud may refuse to open when you get them home.

The choice

For goodness sake choose a plant that will enjoy living with you. Don't check its requirements *after* you've bought it; look at the following lists *before* you buy to find the right plant for the corner you want to fill.

For unheated rooms Adiantum (maidenhair fern), Araucaria (Norfolk Island pine), Aspidistra, Beloperone (shrimp plant), Billbergia (queen's tears), Browallia, Calceolaria (slipper flower), Campanula, Chlorophytum (spider plant), Chrysanthemum, Citrus (orange), Cordyline, Cyclamen, Cytisus (broom), Erica (Cape heath),

Fatshedera, Fatsia (false castor oil palm), Hedera (ivy), Hydrangea, Pelargonium (geranium), Primula, Rhododendron (azalea), Rhoicissus (grape ivy), Saxifraga (mother-of-thousands), Senecio (cineraria), Soleirolia (mind-your-own-business, baby's tears).

For centrally-heated rooms Aechmea (urn plant), Aglaeonema, Anthurium (flamingo flower), Aphelandra (zebra plant), Begonia, Chlorophytum (spider plant), Codiaeum (croton, Joseph's coat), Columnea, Dieffenbachia (dumb cane), Dizygotheca (finger aralia), Dracaena (dragon tree), Epipremnum (devil's ivy, scindapsus), Euphorbia (poinsettia), Ficus (fig, rubber plant), Heptapleurum (umbrella tree), Howea (palm), Hoya (wax plant), Maranta (prayer plant), Monstera (Swiss cheese plant), Pandanus (screw pine), Peperomia (pepper plant), Philodendron (sweetheart plant), Pilea (aluminium plant), Plectranthus, Rhoicissus (grape ivy), Saintpaulia (African violet), Sansevieria (mother-in-law's tongue), Schefflera, Sinningia (gloxinia), Stephanotis, Streptocarpus (Cape primrose), Yucca (ti tree).

For shady corners Adiantum (maidenhair fern), Asparagus, Aspidistra, Asplenium (bird's nest fern), Cissus (kangaroo vine), Fatshedera, Fatsia (false castor oil palm), Fittonia (net leaf), Maranta (prayer plant), Nephrolepis (ladder fern), Pellaea (button fern), Peperomia (pepper plant), Philodendron (sweetheart plant), Pilea (aluminium plant), Platycerium (stag's horn fern), Plectranthus, Rhoicissus (grape ivy), Sansevieria (mother-in-law's tongue), Soleirolia (mind-your-own-business, baby's tears).

For windowsills Browallia, Campanula, Capsicum (pepper), Coleus (flame nettle), Crassula, Cryptanthus

Ferns grow well in a warm bathroom – see page 6 for ideas

(earth stars), Cyclamen, Dionaea (Venus' fly trap), Erica (Cape heath), Fuchsia, Hedera (ivy), Impatiens (busy lizzie), Kalanchoe, Nertera (bead plant), Pelargonium (geranium), Plectranthus, Primula, Rhododendron (azalea), Saintpaulia (African violet), Sansevieria (mother-in-law's tongue), Saxifraga (mother of thousands), Schlumbergera (Christmas cactus), Senecio (cineraria), Setcreasea, Solanum (Christmas pepper), Soleirolia (mind-your-own-business, baby's tears), Tradescantia (wandering sailor), Zebrina.

For warm bathrooms Adiantum (maidenhair fern), Aechmea (urn plant), Aglaeonema, Anthurium (flamingo flower), Aphelandra (zebra plant), Asparagus, Asplenium (bird's nest fern), Begonia, Beloperone (shrimp plant), Billbergia (queen's tears), Codiaeum (croton, Joseph's coat), Cryptanthus (earth stars), Cyperus (umbrella grass), Dieffenbachia (dumb cane), Dionaea (Venus' fly trap), Dracaena (dragon tree), Epipremnum (devil's ivy), Fittonia (net leaf), Maranta (prayer plant), Nephrolepis (ladder fern), Pellaea (button fern), Peperomia (pepper plant), Pilea (aluminium plant), Platycerium (stag's horn fern), Plectranthus, Pteris (ribbon fern), Saintpaulia (African violet), Tradescantia (wandering sailor), Zebrina.

Architectural specimen plants Araucaria (Norfolk Island pine), Codiaeum (croton, Joseph's coat), Cordyline, Cycas (cycad), Dizygotheca (finger aralia), Dracaena (dragon tree), Fatsia (false castor oil palm), Ficus (fig, rubber plant), Heptapleurum (umbrella tree), Howea (palm), Monstera (Swiss cheese plant), Pandanus (screw pine), Philodendron (sweetheart plant), Sansevieria (mother-in-law's tongue), Schefflera, Yucca (ti tree).

Climbers for screens and tripods Cissus (kangaroo vine), Epipremnum (devil's ivy), Fatshedera, Hedera (ivy), *Hoya carnosa* (wax plant), Jasminum (white jasmine), Philodendron (sweetheart plant), Rhoicissus (grape ivy), Stephanotis.

Plants that are difficult to kill Asparagus, Beloperone (shrimp plant), Chlorophytum (spider plant), Cissus (kangaroo vine), Cyperus (umbrella grass), Heptapleurum (umbrella tree), Philodendron (sweetheart plant), Plectranthus, Rhoicissus, Sansevieria (mother-in-law's tongue) – except by overwatering, Tradescantia.

Plants at home

Once you've lugged your chosen plant home its battle for survival begins. It *wants* to live, so all you have to do is provide it with reasonable growing conditions.

Unpack the plant as soon as possible and stand it in good light but not brilliant sunshine. Even plants that like full light will appreciate a day's breather to get used to the atmosphere of their new home. If the compost in the pot is dry, soak it thoroughly with tepid water.

After a day or two, put the plant in its permanent spot. If it's being positioned on its own, a pot-hider or saucer will smarten up the container and prevent any drips from marking your Chippendale furniture. Plants grouped together are happiest when stood on a tray of moist gravel which keeps the air around them pleasantly humid.

Keep all house plants out of these deathtraps:

- Near radiators
- In draughts or behind closed curtains at night
- Places where they are constantly knocked.

Fatshedera will grow in an unheated room or shady corner

How much light?

All plants need light, but some can put up with less than others, and these are the ones to choose for your shady corners (see list on page 4).

Most plants enjoy what the experts call 'good, indirect light', which is the kind found 1 to 2m (3 to 6ft) from a window. Some, like pelargoniums (geraniums, to you) and impatiens (busy lizzies) adore full sunlight and will not flower freely in anything else. Plants that become spindly and 'drawn' are almost certainly not getting enough light – even shade lovers need a certain amount of brightness. Hold the book at arm's length in the spot chosen for the plant and try to read this small print:

If you find it impossible to read this, then one of two things is likely: either there is insufficient light to grow even shade-loving plants; or you need a new pair of glasses. Or both.

How much heat?

Most plants prefer to be warm during the day and cool at night; the state of affairs in most homes. But some plants don't enjoy high temperatures at any time and are guaranteed to suffer if kept too warm:

- Cyclamen
- Erica (Cape heath)
- Rhododendron (azalea)
- Senecio (cineraria)

This little lot will grow well only in cool rooms where the temperature hovers around the 13 to 16°C mark (55 to 60°F). That's too cold for most warm-blooded central-heating lovers, so keep these plants in cool halls or bedrooms.

Use the lists on pages 3 and 4 as a guide to find plants that will cope with your heating, or lack of it.

Humidity

Brown-edged leaves are a common sight on lots of house plants and the cause is almost always dry air. There isn't one plant that won't benefit from extra humidity in the home and it's as easy as pie to provide. Simply stand the plant or group of plants on a tray of gravel which can be kept moist at all times. Alternatively fill a deeper dish with moist peat and plunge the pots into it.

Single specimen plants can be sprayed over daily with tepid rainwater from a hand mister, but watch your furniture!

Watering

Ninety-nine per cent of all house plant deaths are caused by overwatering. So be careful! A house plant will quickly recover from wilt due to underwatering; it will seldom recover from wilt due to overwatering.

Humidity can be increased by standing plants in a tray of gravel which is kept moist at all times

Question: How often do I water it?
Answer: When it's dry.
Look at the compost in the pot, then feel it with your fingers. If it's dusty on the surface it's probably dry right the way through. If it feels like a freshly wrung-out flannel then it's still moist.

If you can't see or feel the compost because of the tightly packed foliage, get used to weighing the plant in your hand. When dry it will feel very light.

Peaty composts shrink when they are dry. Watch for a fine crack between the edge of the compost and the pot – don't wait until it turns into a chasm.

When a plant *is* dry, soak it thoroughly from the top, unless you can't fit the spout of your watering can or jug among the rosette of leaves. If this is the case (it's very likely with African violets and cyclamens), stand the plant in a bowl of water for half an hour, then remove it. During that time it will have taken up all the water it needs. Don't water again until the compost is dry once more.

There are four exceptions to the watering rule:

- Bromeliads (pineapple family)
- Cyperus (umbrella grass)
- Ferns
- Rhododendrons (azaleas)

Ferns should be kept slightly moist at all times; rhododendrons and cyperus should be kept very moist. Bromeliads with 'vases' of leaves should always have some water in their vase.

Test your plants for water daily in summer; weekly in winter – they'll require much less water between October and March.

A bromeliad such as *Neoregelia carolinae* 'Tricolor' always needs some water in its 'vase'

Hydroculture

The coward's way out! A hydroculture unit is a reservoir of water over which is suspended a plastic basket of expanded clay granules through which the plant's roots grow. Each unit looks like a plastic box and has a small indicator on the side which shows when the water in the reservoir needs topping up. The plant absorbs all the water it needs, and special liquid fertiliser can be diluted in the water.

The units are bought ready planted and are very easy to manage. Don't confuse them with self-watering pots which contain compost and a series of wicks leading to a reservoir below. I've yet to see a plant growing really well in one of these units, while those in the hydroculture pots seem to thrive.

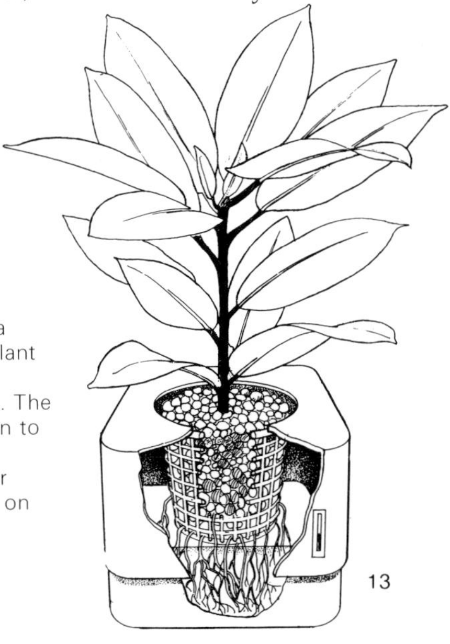

A cut-away diagram of a hydroculture unit. The plant is supported in a basket containing clay granules. The feeding roots grow down to absorb the nutrient-rich water. Note the indicator showing the water level on the right

Feeding

Plants need food as well as drink, but they can only absorb it in liquid form. Diluted liquid feeds can be watered on to the moist compost in the pot once a month from March to October. Only Christmas- and winter-flowering pot plants need be fed between November and February.

Idlers can sprinkle slow-release plant-food granules on to the surface of the compost at any time. These will take a small amount of food to the roots every time the plant is watered.

Pot plant fertiliser is widely available, but all flowering house plants enjoy liquid tomato fertiliser which promotes blooming. Use it at the dilution rate recommended for tomatoes, except on very young plants which will prefer half strength. It works a treat in coaxing flower-shy African violets into bloom.

Foliar feeds can be used on all plants except ferns and those which have hairy leaves. The diluted solution is sprayed on to the foliage, which should be kept out of full sunshine until the spray has dried off.

Newly potted plants will not need feeding for a couple of months.

Pots and compost

Sooner or later the plant you buy is going to need a larger pot and more compost. You can see how it's getting along by carefully turning it upside down and tapping off its pot against a hard surface. If roots can be seen wrapped around the outside of the compost, the plant is 'pot bound'. One or two house plants prefer to be in this state for quite some time – African violets flower well if pot bound and the mother-in-law's tongue (sansevieria) should not be potted on until it cracks its existing pot – but others will enjoy a move to more spacious accommodation once a year.

Spring and summer are the times to 'pot on' your plants. Choose a plastic pot that is 5cm (2in) larger in diameter than the existing one.

There are two basic kinds of compost suitable for pot plants: the soilless type based on peat, and the John Innes composts.

Peat-based composts are:

- Light
- Clean
- Easy to use
- Difficult to re-wet if allowed to dry out
- Lacking in nutrients after six weeks
- Likely to shrink when dry

John Innes composts are:

- Heavy enough to support top-heavy plants
- Easy to moisten when dry
- Retentive of nutrients
- Variable in quality

Newly rooted house plants can be potted in John Innes No.1 potting compost; the majority of house plants in No.2 compost, and the really vigorous types in No.3 compost which contains most fertiliser. Peat-based compost are suitable for a wide range of plants.

Water the plant thoroughly the day before repotting it. When you're ready to pot, this is what to do:

1. Spread a layer of compost in the base of the pot
2. Knock the plant from its pot and sit it in the new one
3. Feed in compost around the rootball

(a) Knock the plant out of its old pot
(b) Set it in the new pot on a bed of compost
(c) Add compost around the root ball, firming as you go

a

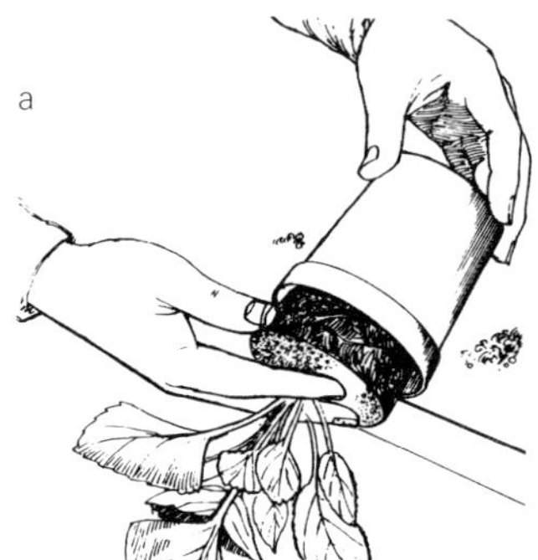

b

c

4. Firm it with your fingers (lightly if it's peat-based)
5. Add more compost until the pot is full
6. When the job is finished the surface of the compost should be 1 to 2cm ($\frac{1}{2}$ to 1in) below the rim of the pot
7. Water the plant by standing it in a bowl of water until the surface of the compost is evenly moist.

Plants in very large pots can be topdressed each spring instead of being potted on. Scrape away 5 to 8cm (2 to 3in) of compost on the surface and replace it with fresh.

Cleaning up

Just like the rest of your furniture, house plants get dusty. They need light if they are to thrive, and a layer of grime prevents the sun from reaching the leaf surfaces. Flick a feather duster over them if you like, but they'll be more effectively cleaned with a tissue or piece of kitchen roll dipped in rainwater or a mixture of equal parts of water and milk (which seems to give them added lustre).

The new 'leaf-shine wipes' which can be bought in small drums with a flip-top are very efficient, but it's a good idea to test both these and aerosol leaf cleaners on a single leaf before treating the entire plant. Never use leaf-cleaning chemicals on:

- Hairy-leaved plants
- Ferns

Ferns are happy being washed clean with a spray of rainwater; hairy-leaved plants such as African violets should be brushed free of dust with a clean paintbrush.

Clean the leaves of your house plants regularly

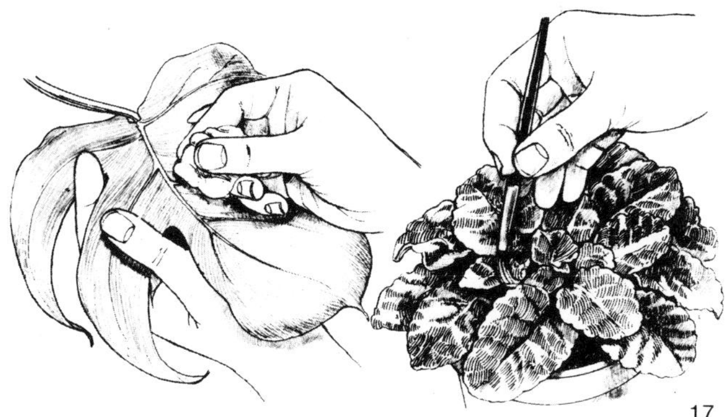

Holding up

Single-stemmed plants can be supported with a single cane and loops of soft twine. Bushy plants can be held up either with small twiggy branches pushed among the foliage, or by a trio of split green canes encircled with twine to form an enclosure. If the plants seem tough enough to support themselves, let them do so.

Plants such as monstera and philodendron are often supported by moss-covered sticks. These are the very devil to keep moist and will usually shed their moss on to your carpet. Replace them with stout canes if necessary, and lead any aerial roots into the compost within the pot.

Climbing plants can have their stems trained up tripods of canes, or over pieces of trelliswork fastened to walls. Stephanotis is often trained around a hoop of wire so that its flowers are shown off well, but it will be equally happy on a tripod.

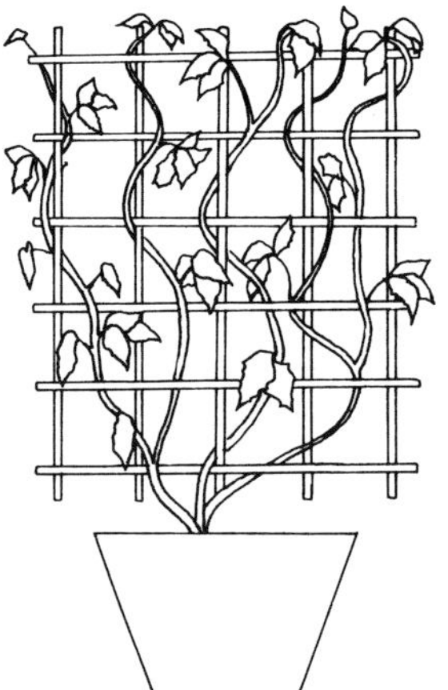

Climbing plants need support

Shaping up

Some house plants need a bit of pruning to keep them shapely and within bounds. Bushy plants that have a tendency to become lanky or 'leggy' should have their shoot tips pinched out regularly (but bear in mind that you may lose flower buds if you do the job too frequently). Vine-like climbers such as:

- Cissus
- Hedera (ivy)
- Philodendron
- Rhoicissus

can be thinned from time to time and whole stems removed. Do the job in spring for preference; at any time of year if you're desperate.

Large plants with one or two stems that look like taking over the house can be mercilessly hacked back in spring. Cut them back to just above a healthy leaf and new shoots will soon sprout. This treatment is suitable for:

- Fatsia
- Ficus (rubber plant)
- Heptapleurum
- Monstera
- Schefflera

Bushy plants that are tired or brown can sometimes be chopped off right at compost level in spring, repotted and allowed to grow again. Try the trick with:

- Adiantum
- Asparagus
- Beloperone
- Campanula
- Coleus
- Impatiens
- Nephrolepis
- Pelargonium
- Plectranthus
- Primula

On holiday

The most reliable form of holiday care for house plants comes in the form of a green-fingered neighbour who can be left with instructions. Failing this good fortune you'll have to make alternative arrangements.

Plants watered well and plunged in plastic seed trays filled with moist peat will often go for two weeks without water if they are kept in a cool room that receives no direct sunlight.

Alternatively you can try capillary watering. This flashy term is used to describe the passage of water from a piece of nylon matting up through the compost in the pot. Here's what to do:

This capillary watering system is a good way of ensuring your plants don't dry out while you are away

1. Place a washing-up bowl in the sink and fill it with water.
2. Lead a piece of capillary matting (sold by garden centres) from the bowl up on to the draining board.
3. Stand the plants on the matting.
4. Check that it is moist before you leave.

Hey presto! The plants should drink what they want while you're away.

Remember that this scheme only works with plants in plastic pots. Plants in clay pots should be provided with wicks – short lengths of the matting material – to bridge the gap between the base of the compost and the mat.

Another watering system particularly suited to clay pots; note the wick leading from the pot to the water bath

Problem pages

Even the most greenfingered of indoor gardeners has a few greenfly now and again, and there are other pests and diseases that will make your life a misery. Don't worry. Take the right action promptly and your plants should soon recover. But the main causes for concern are things called physiological disorders. They're not caused by a pest or a disease but by you or your home environment. Either you're growing the plant in the wrong place, or you're doing something that upsets it.

Do your Sherlock Holmes bit to find out just what's wrong – it could be one of several things – and when you've pinpointed the culprit, take the recommended action.

Here's what might go wrong.

Leaves turning yellow If only one or two of the older

Dry out an overwatered plant by standing it, minus its pot, on a wad of newspaper

leaves low down on the plant are going yellow, it's nothing more than old age or 'natural senescence'.

Plants like the weeping fig (*Ficus benjamina*) and the umbrella tree (*Heptapleurum arboricola*) will often produce a good few yellow leaves just after they've been bought and these usually fall off, too. Don't move the plants (provided they're in a suitable spot). They'll soon recover.

If a plant has a number of leaves that are turning yellow and the above suggestions do not apply, suspect one of the following:

- Overwatering – let the compost dry out between waterings
- Shortage of light – move the plant near to a window
- Shortage of nutrients – feed the plant monthly in summer
- Draughts – move the plant

Leaves brown at the tips Brown leaf tips show that the plant is unable to circulate sap to the extremities of the leaf due to unfavourable conditions. Guard against:

- Dry air – stand the plant on a tray of moist gravel
- Draughts – move the plant
- Scorch from a radiator – keep the plant at least 1.25m (4ft) from a heat source
- Underwatering – aim to keep the compost slightly moist but not constantly soggy

Leaves spotted with brown Sunken brown blotches appear at random on the surface of otherwise healthy leaves. In most cases the cause will be dryness of the air around the plant due to sun scorch. If the plant sits in a brilliant window, move it to more indirect light.

Hairy-leaved plants such as African violets (saint-

Brown tipped yellowing leaves due to scorch and draughts

paulias) and gloxinias develop brown patches when water is splashed on the leaves. Avoid this by watering them from below.

If neither of these causes is to blame, suspect underwatering, or the reverse – overwatering – and take the appropriate action.

Check, the plant for any signs of pests.

Flower bud drop Just when the buds are fattening and beginning to show colour, off they drop, never to open. The plant has received some kind of check due to one of the following circumstances:

- Dryness at the roots – keep the compost evenly moist, but not soggy, when flower buds are developing
- Dry air – stand the plant on a gravel tray in centrally heated rooms
- Draughts – move the plant carefully (see below)
- Movement of the plant – Christmas cacti and fuchsias will often shed their flowers if they are moved from cool to warm temperatures, or vice-versa, while the blooms are forming
- Lack of light – move the plant into a brighter spot if it's in shade

No flowers produced The plant's obviously not in the right frame of mind to produce blooms and it's up to you to give it conditions conducive to flowering. If the plant has been overpotted (given too large a container full of fresh compost) it will probably be so busy making roots that it has no inclination to make flowers.

Alternatively, if it hasn't been fed for months it could simply be too starved to make the effort. Tomato fertiliser (diluted as instructed for tomatoes) will often coax flower-shy plants into full bloom. It's especially good on African violets (saintpaulias). If neither of these reasons apply, suspect:

- Lack of light – move the plant to a brighter spot
- Unsuitable temperatures – is the plant too warm or too cold?

Leaf fall The plant is unhappy and feels that, under the present circumstances, it hasn't the energy to keep all its leaves alive, so it sheds them. There are several reasons why this might happen:

- Overwatering – let the compost dry out between waterings
- Underwatering – try to keep the compost evenly moist, but not soggy
- Draughts – move the plant
- Sudden changes in temperature – have you recently moved the plant? Has there been a power cut? Has the weather turned warmer or colder?

Spindly shoots Plants develop long and 'drawn' shoots for one reason only – they are short of light. Plants such as pelargoniums (often called geraniums) turn pale and spindly very quickly unless kept on a sunny windowsill. Move any spindly plant into a brightly lit spot.

Stem rotting The rotting of any plant tissue is caused by fungus diseases, and fungus diseases only thrive in moist situations. You're keeping the plant too wet at the roots. Allow it to dry out a little between waterings – if it's not too late to save it. Dusting lightly affected areas with a fungicide powder will help to stop the rot.

Variegation fading If the brightly variegated leaves of your ivies, or umbrella tree (*Heptapleurum arboricola* 'Variegata') or any other plant are fading, the cause is almost certain to be lack of light. Move the plant to a brightly lit spot and the variegation should return.

Every now and then an otherwise healthy variegated plant will throw out a plain green shoot. This is a reversion to its original form. Snip out such shoots completely and the plant should continue to produce more variegated ones.

Wilting Leaves of healthy plants are stiff or 'turgid' due to the flow of sap in the leaves and the presence of water. If the leaves wilt it's likely that the plant is in a state of shock and unable to keep pumping round the sap with its usual vigour. It will wilt for one of several reasons:

- Overwatering – you can let the plant dry out but it will seldom recover
- Underwatering – soak the compost and the plant will usually pick up; it's always best to underwater rather than overwater
- Sun scorch – move the plant into a spot that's indirectly lit

If none of these is the case, tap the plant from its pot and look for root pests. Vine weevil grubs are the most likely cause of wilting. They are small, fat, creamy maggots which eat the roots. Precious plants that are only slightly affected can either be watered with dilute HCH, or they can have all the compost washed off their roots and be repotted carefully in sterile compost. It's better, though, to ditch any affected plant, for if the grubs spread to other house plants the results could be disastrous.

Vine weevil is an especial problem on cyclamen.

Leaves coated with white powder When you've made sure that it's neither dust nor talcum powder you

Leaf miner damage on chrysanthemum – see page 31

can be fairly certain that it's mildew. This is a fungus disease that attacks plant leaves. It's more prevalent in a humid atmosphere so, if possible, move the plant to a more airy room. Spray the plant with Benlate and, if the stems are overcrowded, thin them out with a pair of secateurs to improve air circulation.

Black felt-like growth on leaves It looks dreadful but it's really quite easy to get rid of. It's called sooty mould and it's a fungus that grows on the sticky honeydew secreted by aphids (greenfly). First of all, kill off the aphids with a specific aphicide containing a pirimicarb. Take the plant outdoors to spray it and let the solution dry off. Now sponge off the sooty mould with a damp cloth – it will come off a glossy-leaved plant clean as a whistle and the plant will be returned to the peak of health. It's a tedious job though!

Leaves distorted and mottled Unless the variegation is a part of their attraction, plants that have mottled and twisted leaves are infected with undesirable virus diseases. There's no cure. Be hard hearted and ditch the plants in the dustbin. If they are allowed to survive the disease may spread to healthy plants. Viruses are spread by greenfly, so control the pest to control the disease.
Stems or leaves coated with grey fur It's usually during the darker months of the year, or during wet weather, that 'grey mould' appears on leaves and stems. If a leaf dies for any reason, it won't be long before this fungus disease (more properly known as botrytis) attacks it. Pelargoniums (geraniums) are often disfigured by it, especially when they are taken as cuttings – that blackening at soil level (blackleg) will soon be followed by the grey mould that looks like a fur coat.

Like all fungi, this one thrives in a humid atmosphere. Keep plants slightly drier at the roots in winter, and make sure that there's a good circulation of air around them. Pick off any leaves as soon as they start to fade, and any faded flowers, too. Plants which seem prone to the disease can be sprayed with captan.
Greenfly Everybody knows greenfly, but remember that they come in assorted colours – pink, yellow, black and brown as well as green. Spray them with a specific aphicide (an insecticide that won't kill ladybirds, bees and lacewings). Choose one based on pirimicarb.

If you're inclined to be soft-hearted and leave greenfly alone, think again – they weaken the plant by sucking its sap, they transmit crippling virus diseases, and they secrete sticky honeydew that is rapidly colonised by sooty mould. It's not worth having them. If you hate insecticides, brush the bugs off the plant at regular intervals with a dry paint brush, but they'll rapidly return.

Whitefly Unlike greenfly, which only take off when they've exhausted their food supply, whitefly have wings which they use regularly. Tap the leaf and those miniature Concorde-shaped flies will zoom around in circles. They affect the plant in exactly the same way as greenfly but are rather more difficult to kill off because the youngsters are tiny scales that seem immune to most insecticides. Spray with bioresmethrin and repeat the application as recommended on the bottle to control adults which will emerge from the resistant scales. Two or three sprays may be necessary to effect a complete control.

Scale insects These are the barnacles of the plant pest world. They cling to the stems and leaves, especially on glossy-leaved plants such as orange plants and bird's nest ferns (*Asplenium nidus*). They look like tiny brown limpets. Dab them with a paintbrush dipped in methylated spirits, or spray the plant with malathion. The trouble is that ferns are very sensitive to chemicals and you'd be well advised to gently wash the scales off them with damp cottonwool. They suck sap and secrete honeydew just like aphids.

Mealy bugs These are closely related to scale insects and are just as tricky to control. They do move (but very slowly) and are coated in a white, waxy wool. They usually colonise leaf axils and other nooks and crannies. Treat them the same as scale insects.

Red spider mites No. These are not those tiny red spiders you see running about on windowsills. Red spider mites are, for a start, brown or yellowish in colour and about the size of a pin-prick. They colonise plants in a dry atmosphere, sucking sap and bleaching the foliage so that it becomes yellowish and crisp. Examine the undersides of the leaf and you'll find masses of minute specks running around. In severe outbreaks tiny webs are spun over the leaves.

These mites are discouraged by a moist atmosphere, so prevent attacks by standing susceptible plants on trays of moist gravel. Spraying the foliage with tepid water also helps prevent their establishment. Spray any outbreaks with systemic insecticides – varying the product from time to time so that the pest doesn't build up a resistance.

Leaf miners These are the pests that cause those little white ribbon-like scars to be produced on the leaves of chrysanthemums and cinerarias (senecio). The scars are actually tunnels made by the grub which chews its way between the upper and lower leaf surfaces. Pick off badly infected leaves and spray the plant with fenitrothion.

Vine weevils (See wilting, page 27) In minor attacks, the pot can be watered with a dilute solution of HCH. Otherwise, the dustbin is the best place for the casualty.

Dab scale insects with a brush dipped in methylated spirits

Index

Page numbers in italics refer to illustrations